LaGG Fighters

in action

By Hans-Heiri Stapfer

Color by Don Greer & Ernesto Cumpian

Illustrated by Joe Sewell

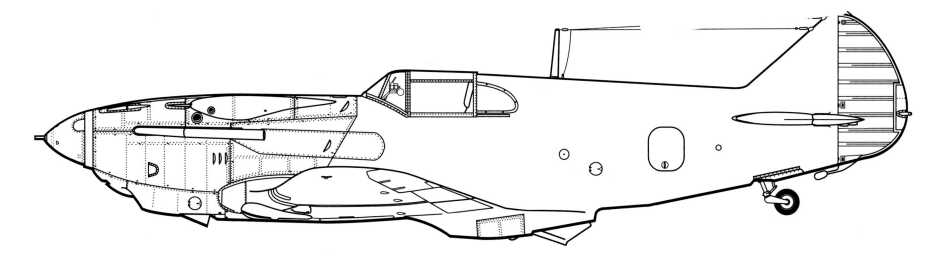

Aircraft Number 163

squadron/signal publications

A LaGG-3 (35th Series) was engaged by Curtiss Hawk 75As of the Finnish Air Force on 14 September 1942. During the action, the LaGG-3 was damaged and made a forced landing on Finnish territory. The aircraft was captured, repaired and put into service with the Finnish Air Force as LG-3.

Acknowledgements

Ivan Ivanov

Robert Gretzyngier

Hannu Valtonen

Carl-Fredrik Geust

Lennart Andersson

Keski-Suomen Ilmailumuseo

Nigel A. Eastaway

Wolfgang Tamme

Hadtorteneti Muzeum

R.A.R.T.

Nicholas J. Waters III

Robert Bock

Mariusz Zimny

Andrzej Morgala

Heinz J. Nowarra

Ivo Zetik

James W. Crow

Frieder Voigt

George Punka

Attila Bonhardt

S.H.A.A.

ISBN 0-89747-634-7

If you have any photographs of aircraft, armor, soldiers or ships of any nation, particularly wartime snapshots, why not share them with us and help make Squadron/Signal's books all the more interesting and complete in the future. Any photograph sent to us will be copied and the original returned. The donor will be fully credited for any photos used. Please send them to:

Squadron/Signal Publications, Inc.
1115 Crowley Drive
Carrollton, TX 75011-5010

Если у вас есть фотографии самолётов, вооружения, солдат или кораблей любой страны, особенно, снимки времён войны, поделитесь с нами и помогите сделать новые книги издательства Эскадрон/Сигнал ещё интереснее. Мы переснимем ваши фотографии и вернём оригиналы. Имена приславших снимки будут сопровождать все опубликованные фотографии. Пожалуйста, присылайте фотографии по адресу:

Squadron/Signal Publications, Inc.
1115 Crowley Drive
Carrollton, TX 75011-5010

軍用機、装甲車両、兵士、軍艦などの写真を所持しておられる方はいらっしゃいませんか？どの国のものでも結構です。作戦中に撮影されたものが特に良いのです。Squadron/Signal社の出版する刊行物において、このような写真は内容を一層充実し、興味深くすることができます。当方にお送り頂いた写真は、複写の後お返しいたします。出版物中に写真を使用した場合は、必ず提供者のお名前を明記させて頂きます。お写真は下記にご送付ください。

Squadron/Signal Publications, Inc.
1115 Crowley Drive
Carrollton, TX 75011-5010

A LaGG-3 (11st Series) of the 5th Guards Fighter Aviation Regiment prepares for take off on a ground attack mission in the Moscow area during February of 1942. This aircraft was armed with six RS-82 rockets. (Ivan Ivanov)

Introduction

The LaGG-3 was one of a trio of modern fighters which had been developed under emergency conditions by the Soviets to replace the obsolete standard Soviet Air Force fighters - the Polikarpov I-16 and I-153. For the Kremlin it was a race against the time, since it had become clear that Adolf Hitler would sooner or later fulfill his dream of having *Lebensraum* (living space) in the East, beyond Soviet borders.

The first LaGG-3s reached Fighter Aviation Regiments in limited numbers during 1941 - just a few months before the German attack (22 June 1941). The LaGG-3 fought in every major campaign, from the Caucasus in the South to the Baltic Sea in the North and many Soviet aces claimed their first kills flying the LaGG-3.

The LaGG-3 was soon outclassed by the more advanced Yakovlev fighter series, but a total of 6,528 aircraft had left the State Aircraft Factories before production ended in September of 1943. Based on numbers built, the LaGG-3 was one of the most successful fighter designs built during the first year of the War.

In the mid-twenties, Iosif Stalin ruthlessly pushed the industrialization of the Soviet Union, and production figures for aircraft increased dramatically. In 1930, the country produced some 860 aircraft, just two years later, production was sufficient to give the Air Force a strength of 2,500 front-line combat aircraft. One of the ways in which this extraordinary increase was achieved was by the use of forced labor. In so called *Sharashkas*, secret research institutes, aircraft were developed by imprisoned scientists and designers.

When the first I-16 monoplane fighter left the assembly lines during late 1934, it was by far the most advanced fighter aircraft in the world, with a high top speed, superior rate of climb and outstanding maneuverability. The development of modern fighters, however, came to a standstill and during 1940, the Soviet Union still produced the biplane Polikarpov I-153 in large numbers.

In the late 1930s, combat reports coming from Spain, revealed that the Messerschmitt Bf-109B and the Bf-109E easily outclassed the I-16 and I-15. This led to a requirement issued, in January 1939, by Stalin and the NKAP (Commissariat of the People for the Aviation Industry) for a new type of a general purpose fighter. Ten design groups, including Polikarpov, Sukhoi and Yakovlev participated in the design competition.

A small design group formed by Semyon Alekseevich Lavochkin, Vladimir Petrovich Gorbunov and Mikhail Ivanovich Gudkov had been working since 1938 on a fighter constructed mostly from wood and decided to submit this design into the competition.

The participating design teams were under a severe time limitation. Considering the Third Reich as a very real threat, Stalin wanted the new fighters in the briefest possible time. The LaGG-3 prototype first flew in March of 1940, barely fourteen months after the project specifications had been issued by the Kremlin. The LaGG-3 prototype was followed a short time later by the MiG fighter prototype (I-200) on 5 April and the Yakovlev prototype (I-26) on 27 April of the same year.

In order not only to overcome the lag in modern fighter development, but also the lag in aviation industry modernization, the Politburo ordered the construction of nine new aircraft factories in September of 1939, with a deadline for completion of two years. Production leapt, although new models, such as the Yak-1, MiG-3 and the LaGG-3 did not became available in substantial numbers until the Spring of 1941. Such forced output, however, took its toll. The quality of aircraft produced was often inferior, with an increase in equipment failures and crashes. Stalin naturally accused Air Force personnel of sabotage.

A remarkable aspect in the development of the LaGG-3 was that, besides Lavochkin, the two other founding members of the design bureau, Gorbunov and Gudkov had never designed an aircraft before. The story of the LaGG-3 actually started in an environment far from aviation. In 1935, Lavochkin was assigned to the Main Administration of the Northern Sea Route where he worked with O.F. Kaplyur in building boats from *Kaplyurit* - plastified wood and plywood armored with steel net. That same year, L. I. Rizhkov, developed delta wood technology. This was a plastified wood and plywood merged with another wood plastic technology: bakelite and balenit. Delta wood was made of layers of birch strips which were glue cross-grained, impregnated and used in conjunction with a bakelite ply.

Delta wood had twice as much volume as simple wood, but promised definite advantages in such load bearing structural elements such as wing spar flanges, fuselage longerons and others. During this time, the Soviet Union faced difficulties in getting high quality wood in great quantities. Experimental spars made of delta wood were produced in the Spring of 1939 for strength tests.

Delta wood was an advanced material also from the point of economy. Especially since the Soviet Union was deficient in duraluminium and other light alloys. In 1938, V. P. Gorbunov and Lavochkin suggested to the Aviation Industry People's Commissar, an idea for building a fighter from this material. This was agreed to and in May of 1938, an experimental shop was allocated for the design work on the new fighter. The team was headed by Gorbunov. Lavochkin and Gudkov were appointed as managers of the experimental shop, which was, in its first months of existence, located in facilities of the Rizhkov OKB. The designation I-22 (I for *Istrebitel*/Fighter) was given to the project.

In May of 1939, the small experimental shop was expanded to an Experimental Design Bureau, called OKB-301, and moved to State Aircraft Factory 301 at Khimki. To assist the design team, a number of experienced engineers from the closed Silvansky OKB were transferred to OKB-301 in the Summer of 1939. During the Great Patriotic War, Lavochkin became the head of the OKB, while Gorbunov and Gudkov, one after the other, left.

The second I-301 prototype during flight testing with the Flight Research Institute at Zhukovsky Air Base in November of 1940. One of the difference between it and production LaGG-3s, was that the I-301 had no landing light in the port wing leading edge. (Ivan Ivanov)

I-22 Prototype

The design proposals formulated at OKB-301 excited enthusiasm, not only because of its projected performance, its excellent drag-weight ratio, but also because its construction demanded a minimum of strategic materials which were lacking in the Soviet Union.

In order to fulfill the task of developing the I-22 as quickly as possible, A.G. Brunov and V.V. Kondratyev were transferred from GAZ-301 to OKB-301, where they worked under Lavochkin. A short time later, a number of specialists from the Bureau for New Designs joined the team. They included D. P. Grigorovich, and Y. B. Sturtzel (who was responsible for the wing design). A substantial amount of airframe development was done by the *TsAGI* (Central Aero Hydrodynamics Institute) at Zhukovsky. Wind tunnels models of the I-22 were tested and, based on these results, corrections were made on the design blue prints.

The I-22 emerged as a single seat, low tapered wing fighter of wooden structure, with most of the materials being birch plywood and pine. Type DSP-10 delta wood was used in the wing spar flanges, ribs and in separate members of forward fuselage. Due to its delta wood construction, the I-22 prototype was, at 6,543 pounds (2,968 kg), considerably heavier than some of its competitors. The Yakovlev I-26, for instance, weighed only 5, 952 pounds (2,700 kg).

The I-22 was powered by a 1,050 hp Klimov M-105P liquid-cooled inline engine driving a VISh-61P three blade, constant speed propeller. Its armament consisted of a pair of 12.7MM Berezin UBS machine guns in the forward fuselage decking with 230 rounds per gun and a PTB-23 23MM cannon with 81 rounds mounted between the engine cylinder banks. The PTB-23 weapon, however, proved unreliable and was replaced by a 12.7MM machine gun.

On 30 March 1940, the prototype took off for its maiden flight with Aleksei I. Nikashin at the controls. The factory test trials were not without problems and several incidents occurred, including at least one crash landing. After solving all the problems detected during the factory testing, the I-22 was transferred to the Flight Research Institute at Zhukovsky for state acceptance trials. Subsequently the prototype was ferried to the Scientific Research Institute of the Soviet Air Force, where a specific Air Force qualification test program was conducted.

The I-22 had a fuel capacity of 89.8 gallons (340 liters), which was housed in three fuselage tanks. It was found during the state acceptance trials that this fuel capacity gave the prototype a range of 372.8 miles (600 km). By that time, the NKAP had issued new orders stating that all new fighter designs must have a range of at least 621 miles (1,000 km). Apart from this shortcoming, the State Acceptance trials showed that the I-22 prototype met all the specifications issued by the NKAP.

I-301 Prototype

In order to increase the fuel capacity of the fighter, the prototype was returned to OKB-301 for modifications. Two wing fuel tanks were installed, which increased the fuel capacity to 119 gallons (452 liters) and gave the fighter an endurance of 2.5 hours. In addition, an aft sliding canopy was installed. In its original configuration, the prototype had no canopy.

Under the designation I-301, the prototype was sent back for state acceptance trials on 14 June 1940. During the evaluation trials, the I-301 reached a speed of 312.5 mph (503 km/h) at ground level and 376 mph (605 km/h) at 16,404 feet (5,000 meters). At this altitude, the I-301 was 12.42 mph (20 km/h) faster than the Yakovlev I-26. It had a rate of climb of 2,929 feet

per minute, but due to its heavy weight, the I-301 had a ceiling of only 31,496 feet (9,600 meters) while the I-26 had a ceiling of 33,464 feet (10,200 meters) and the I-200 fighter from the MiG design bureau had a ceiling of 39,370 feet (12,000 meters). Because of its shiny, highly polished skin, the prototype was nicknamed the "Piano".

On 11 February 1940, an agreement with Germany guaranteed it raw materials from the Soviet Union. In return, Germany shipped, beside other military equipment, five Messerschmitt Bf-109E-3 fighters to Russia in May of 1940. During their testing, it was discovered that the Messerschmitt Bf-109E-3 far outclassed Soviet standard fighters. The I-16 was almost 62 mph (100 km/h) slower and the I-153 biplane was more than 100 km/h slower.

During this test program a number of evaluation flights were conducted between the I-301, and a Messerschmitt Bf-109B-1 (which had been captured in Spain) and the Messerschmitt Bf-109E-3s. At 16,000 feet (5,000 meter), the Messerschmitt Bf-109E-3 was remarkable slower (339 mph/546 km/h) than the I-301 (376 mph/605 km/h). The I-301 could also out-turn Bf-109E-3. On the last day of the evaluation, the I-301 made an endurance flight from Moscow to Kursk and back. As the prototype touched down there was still some 15 percent fuel remaining in its tanks.

Although the I-301 had stiff ailerons and elevators and a number of other disadvantages, the type was accepted for mass production on 29 July 1940. A second prototype of the I-301 became available in November of 1940, after the end of the state acceptance trials. This aircraft incorporated all the modifications done on the first prototype during the evaluation.

The political situation in Europe did not allow for a general revision of the design which might have improved the flying characteristics and performance of the I-301. The *Blitzkrieg* had been launched and, just a short time later, in May of 1940, France, Belgium and Holland were overrun by the German Panzer forces.

Even with the Non-Aggression Pact signed with Germany on 23 August 1939, the Kremlin knew it was just a matter of time before Germany attacked the Soviet Union. The Soviet Air Force needed large quantities of modern fighters that could match the Messerschmitt Bf-109 as quickly as possible, fighters such as the I-301.

No radio was carried on the second prototype and it also lacked the rudder balance weights, which were introduced on production LaGG-3s. The second I-301 was armed with three Berezin UBS 12.7MM machine guns. (Ivan Ivanov)

Development

I-301 Prototype

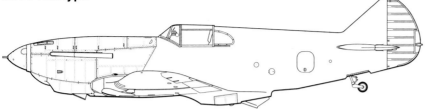

LaGG-3 1st Series

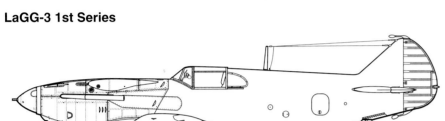

LaGG-3 4th Series

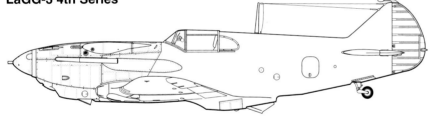

LaGG-3 11th Series

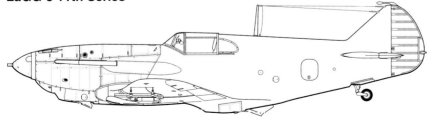

LaGG-3 23rd Series

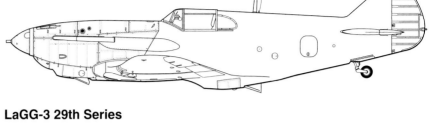

LaGG-3 29th Series

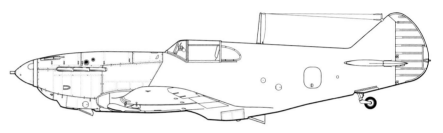

LaGG-3 35th Series

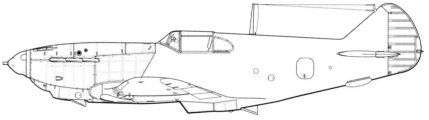

LaGG-3 66th Series

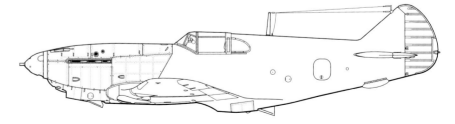

LaGG-3 (1st Series)

The Eighteenth Party Conference of February 1941, four months before the German attack on the Soviet Union, was devoted almost entirely to defense matters. The budget allocation for defense during the period 1928 to 1933 had been only 5.4 per cent of the gross national product, by 1941, this figure had risen to 43.4 per cent. From early 1940 to 22 June 1941, the day of the German invasion, a total of 2,829 modern fighters and bombers had been built, including 1,289 MiG-3s, 399 Yak-1s and 322 LaGG-3s.

On 29 July 1940, the I-301 was cleared for mass production. Four State Aircraft Factories were selected for initial production: GAZ-21 (GAZ = *Gosudarstvenny Aviatsionny Zavod*/State Aircraft Factory) at Nizhny-Novgorod, GAZ-23 at Leningrad, GAZ-31 at Taganrog and GAZ-153 at Novosibirsk.

In December of 1940, the Soviet Air Force designation I-301 was replaced by the designation, LaGG-3, which honored its designers: S. A. Lavochkin, V. P. Gorbunov and M. I. Gudkov.

A month before, in November of 1940, Lavochkin was sent to GAZ-21 and Gorbunov to

This early LaGG-3 (1st Series) crash-landed at State Aircraft Factory 21 on 16 May 1941. It was equipped with a tall antenna mast on the fuselage and a stub antenna on the fin, but lacks the rudder balance weights. These were typical features for very early production LaGG-3s. (Ivan Ivanov)

GAZ-31, where both men were to supervise LaGG-3 production. Gudkov remained at OKB-301, with a few assistants, where he continued work on several other projects.

The vast State Aircraft Factory 301, where the OKB-301 was located, never built the LaGG-3. Instead, it produced Yak-1s, with initial production beginning in May of 1941. Four to five aircraft a day were produced, but the quality of the Yak-1s and Yak-7s produced here was

White 14, an early LaGG-3 (1st Series) lines up takeoff on a mission over the Leningrad front in the Autumn of 1941, shortly before Leningrad was besieged by the Wehrmacht. There are patches from earlier repairs on the fin. The canopy was removed, a common practice on early LaGG-3s, since the canopy could not be jettisoned. (Ivan Ivanov)

Workers prepare to add skinning to the rear fuselage of a LaGG-3 (1st Series). With the skinning removed, the delta wood structure of the fighter is visible. The small radio mast was a typical feature found on LaGG-3 (1st Series) fighters. (Robert Bock)

inferior and many tailwheels of Khimki assembled aircraft failed after some fourteen landings. GAZ-301 soon earned the reputation for poor quality standards before the factory was uprooted and moved east of the Ural Mountains after the German attack.

Production of the new LaGG fighter did not progress smoothly, since the aircraft and its drawings were "raw" and not really fully developed for series production. In addition, it soon turned out that the LaGG-3, with its delta wood technology, was much more complex than a conventional design, such as the Polikarpov I-16 and I-153, which had preceded the LaGG-3 on the production lines. Many workers in the four State Aircraft Factories were totally unqualified in this type of work and had no prior professional contact with aeronautical tech-

A LaGG-3 (1st Series) runs up its engine as it is prepared for a mission. The propeller was painted White and the muzzle of the engine mounted Berezin UBS 12.7mm machine gun is visible in the center of the spinner. (Robert Bock)

Fuselage Development

I-301 Prototype

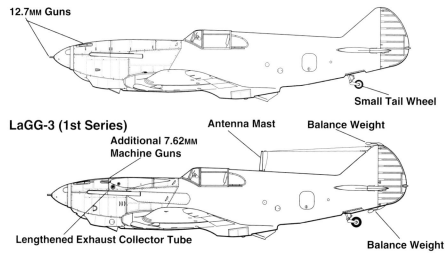

12.7mm Guns

Small Tail Wheel

LaGG-3 (1st Series)

Antenna Mast   Balance Weight

Additional 7.62mm Machine Guns

Lengthened Exhaust Collector Tube

Balance Weight

nology.

For these reasons, production of the LaGG-3 started very slowly and the first aircraft were not delivered until January of 1941. Not all factories began building the new fighter at the same time, for instance, the 30,000 engineers and workers of GAZ-21, were still converting from the Polikarpov I-16 Type 29 to the LaGG-3 on 22 June 1941. As a result of their inexperience with the LaGG-3, the daily production rate at the facility had reached only six aircraft by the Summer 1941.

There were a number of differences between the I-301 prototype and the standard production LaGG-3. There were two flush type gun ports for the Berezin UBS 12.7mm machine guns on the nose of the I-301. These gun ports were slightly modified on the production LaGG-3. The exhaust collector tube was lengthened and the air intake on both sides above the carburetor intake was enlarged. The small blister on top of the wing root on the I-301 was deleted on production LaGG-3s.

No radio was carried on the I-301 prototype, while production LaGG-3s had provision for a radio, although the RSI-3 *Orel* (RSI=*Radiostancija dlja Istrebitelei*/Radio for fighter) radio transmitter/receiver was not carried on all aircraft. The introduction of a radio resulted in the introduction of an antenna mast on the fuselage spine behind the cockpit. Usually, in a formation, only the lead LaGG-3 was equipped with both, a transmitter and receiver, while the remaining aircraft had either only a receiver or no radio.

In contrast to the Polikarpov I-16 and I-153, which were equipped with a 12 Volt electrical system, the new generation fighters (Yak-1, MiG-3 and LaGG-3) were equipped with a 24 Volt electrical system.

The main landing gear was also modified from the prototype. The main landing gear legs were enlarged and the hinged wheel cover flap attached to the main wheel doors on the prototype was deleted on production LaGG-3s. A blister was on the main landing gear strut on production LaGG-3, which was not found on the I-301 prototype. The tail wheel was also

Ground crewmen prepare a 1st Series LaGG-3 of the 44th Fighter Aviation Regiment for a mission over the Leningrad area. The Red star national insignia on the tail has a thin Black outline. No national markings were carried on the wing upper-surfaces, a common practice in Lavochkin regiments during the war. (Robert Bock)

enlarged in diameter and a fairing was placed over the tail wheel bay to reduce drag.

The I-301 had no landing light, while all production LaGG-3s were equipped with a landing light in the leading edge of the port wing. On the prototype, a single position light was fitted on each wing tip, while production LaGG-3s had two position lights, one on the top and and

During the winter, it was common to remove the lower main landing gear doors to prevent mud and slush from building up on the landing gear. Many pilots had the canopy removed since it could not be jettisoned. (Robert Bock)

one on the bottom of the wing, slightly inboard of the wing tip.

Production LaGG-3s also differed from the I-301 prototype in having increased firepower. Armament included two Berezin UBS 12.7MM machine guns, with a rate of fire of 800 rounds

A pilot leaves his LaGG-3 (1st Series) after a mission in the Leningrad area during late 1941. The small antenna mast was typical for all early production LaGG-3s. Both the tactical number and propeller spinner were in White. (Robert Bock)

A winter camouflaged LaGG-3 (1st Series) of the 44th Fighter Aviation Regiment taxies out for a mission over the Leningrad area. The canopy and the lower main landing gear door have been removed. This LaGG-3 carries a large Red star on the rear fuselage and a small Red star on the rudder. (Robert Bock)

per minute and an ammunition supply of 220 rounds per gun. These guns were installed in the forward fuselage upper decking and an additional Berezin UBS was installed between the engine cylinder banks firing through the propeller hub. Additionally, two ShKAS 7.62MM machine guns were installed in the upper fuselage decking above the engine, covered by large fairings. These guns had a rate of fire of 1,800 rounds per minute, with an ammunition supply of 325 rounds per gun. The additional two guns and their ammunition were responsible for a substantial increase in gross weight when compared with the original I-301 prototype.

LaGG-3s were equipped with a PBP-1 (*Prizel dlya Bombometaniya S Pikirovaniya*/Bomb Sight for Dive Bombing) gun sight, although some later production batches were equipped with an updated PBP-1A sight. The PBP-1 was a reflector type sight with two deflection rings, one for 124 mph (200 km/h) and one for 186 mph (300 km/h). The sight was unable to provide the pilot with a fine degree of deflection and made it necessary to make attacks either head on or tail chase. Based on experience gained in the Spanish civil war with the Polikarpov I-15 and I-16, a 10MM section of armor plate was installed behind the pilot seat.

There were five wing fuel tanks made from aluminum-magnesium alloy overlaid by four layers of phenol-formaldehyde resin-impregnated fabric to make the tanks self-sealing. The LaGG-3 fuel system had a fire suppression system where inert gases were pumped into empty tanks from the port exhaust manifold. The exhaust gases were collected in a tube, which lead to a filter in the rear fuselage. Then, the cooled exhaust gases were transferred to the five tanks. The LaGG-3 was the only modern Soviet fighter using exhaust gasses to suppress fuel fires. The LaGG-3 had an endurance of 2.5 hours for a range of 559 miles (900 km) using an economical cruising speed of 282.7 mph (455 km/h).

The LaGG-3 was about 661 pounds (300 kg) heavier than the Yak-1 fighter. This was due to the fuselage wood structures organic property, in comparison with the composite fuselage structure of the Yakovlev fighters, which turned out considerably lighter.

The LaGG-3 was powered by a 1,100 hp Klimov liquid-cooled 12 cylinder Vee M-105P power plant, a Soviet derivative of the Hispano-Suiza HS 12Y engine. License production of the HS 12 Y had been granted to the Soviet Union and the engine had been built as the M-100 and then modified to the M-105 by Vladimir Y. Klimov and his design team. The M-105P was equipped with a centrifugal two-speed two-stage supercharger for use at low and medium altitudes. The engine drove a VISh-61P three blade, all metal propeller with a R-6 hydraulic pitch control that was especially developed for cannon armed fighters.

Compared with the I-301 prototype, the first production aircraft weighed some154 pounds (70 kg) heavier and had lower top speed, the loss of speed was also a result of drag produced by the poor workmanship of the wing and fuselage skinning, which was not as smooth as the I-301 prototype.

Flight tests performed in May 1941, by pilots of the Scientific Research Institute of the

The wreckage of captured Soviet aircraft were taken to the *Deutsche Versuchsanstalt für Luftfahrt* (Research Center for Aviation) at Berlin-Adlershof for careful examination by German specialists. Based on their research work, technical reports on captured aircraft were issued to front-line units. The Berezin UBS 12.7MM machine gun in the nose was used on LaGG-3s of the first three production series. (Manfred Griehl)

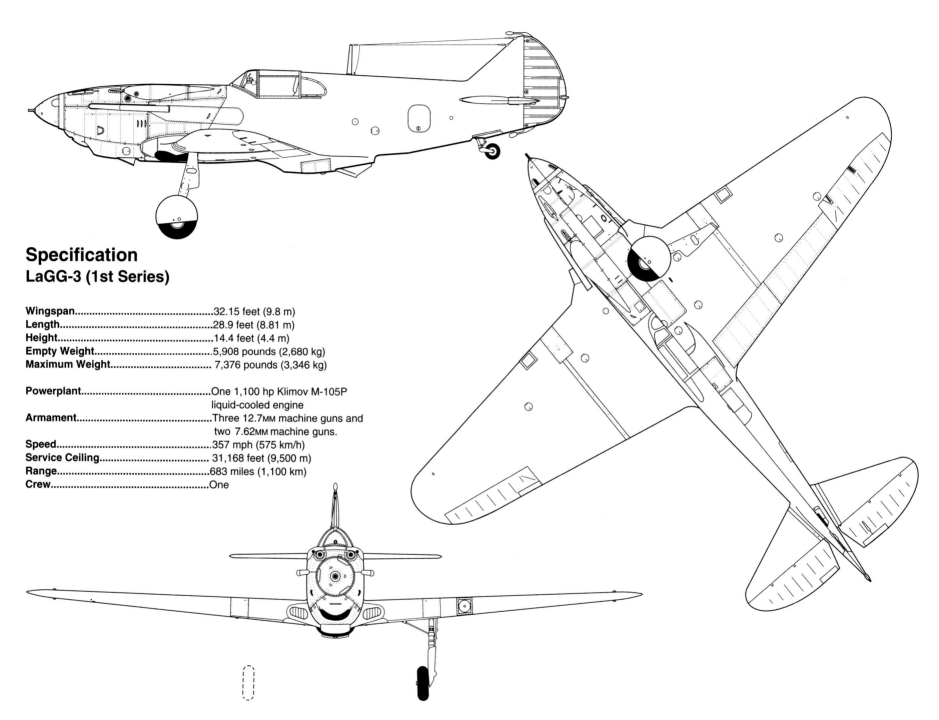

Specification
LaGG-3 (1st Series)

Wingspan..32.15 feet (9.8 m)
Length...28.9 feet (8.81 m)
Height...14.4 feet (4.4 m)
Empty Weight...................................5,908 pounds (2,680 kg)
Maximum Weight.............................. 7,376 pounds (3,346 kg)

Powerplant...One 1,100 hp Klimov M-105P
                                                                 liquid-cooled engine
Armament...Three 12.7мм machine guns and
                                                                 two 7.62мм machine guns.
Speed...357 mph (575 km/h)
Service Ceiling................................... 31,168 feet (9,500 m)
Range...683 miles (1,100 km)
Crew...One

Soviet Air Force at Chalovskaya near Moscow, revealed that the general performance of the standard production LaGG-3 was considerably lower than the I-301 prototype. At sea level the I-301 had a top speed of 320 mph (515 km/h) while the LaGG-3 had a top speed of 303 mph (498 km/h). Speed at altitude dropped from 376 mph (605 km/h) for the I-301 to 357 mph (575 km/h) for the production LaGG-3. The prototype had a rate of climb of 2,804 feet per minute while the production aircraft had a rate of climb of 2,412 feet per minute, in fact a production LaGG-3 could be outclimbed by the Polikarpov I-16, one of the types that it was intended to replace.

The poor elevator control response of the first production LaGG-3s (1st Series) was corrected by the addition of a horn balance weight fitted to the top and bottom of the elevator. Initial production LaGG-3s (1st Series) lacked these balance weights, but most LaGG-3s (1st Series) versions were equipped with the weights on the elevator.

The first pre-series production batches of LaGG-3s (1st Series) built at GAZ-21 were equipped with a tall antenna mast behind the cockpit and an stub antenna mast on the fin. Over the course of production, LaGG-3s (1st Series) were simplified, with the stub mast on the fin being deleted and the antenna mast on the fuselage behind the cockpit being shortened. Most LaGG-3s (1st Series) were built with a small antenna mast, two rudder balance weights

Two damaged LaGG-3 were found by the advancing Wehrmacht on railroad cars. The fighter nearest camera is a LaGG-3 (1st Series). The oval air intakes in the wing root and the lack of an air intake on the port radiator skinning are typical features found on aircraft made in the first three production series. The aircraft in the background is a LaGG-3 (4th Series). (Manfred Griehl)

and no aerial stub on the fin. The tall antenna mast, however, was reintroduced on the LaGG-3 (4th Series), and the stub antenna was once again installed on LaGG-3 of the 23rd Series.

The first three series of the LaGG-3 were (with the exception of the initial production batches at GAZ-21) very similar and differed in small details from each other. Most LaGG-3s of the first three production series had oval induction air intakes, while a few aircraft had triangle shaped induction air intakes.

During the Spring of 1941, initial conversion training of Fighter Aviation Regiments stationed in Soviet Asia was started. This process required time and a great deal of effort. These Fighter Aviation Regiments were based near the border with Mongolia and China. The Soviet Union was engaged in border fighting with Japanese troops on the Manchurian-Mongolian border during the Autumn of 1939 and the Soviet Air Force wanted to equip the units based in the Far Eastern districts with their latest fighter type, in case fighting with the Japanese Kwantung Army flamed up again.

The Finnish Air Force captured a LaGG-3 (1st Series) and based it at Tampere with the registration LG-2. The three piece exhaust stub was an addition to the aircraft taken from the wreck of a LaGG-3 from a later production batch. The small inlet under the first stub on the nose was a typical feature for LaGG-3s of the three production batches. (Keski-Suomen Ilmailumuseo via Hannu Valtonen)

The Finnish Air Force LaGG-3 (Serial Number 0110072) was camouflaged in Black and Olive Green on the uppersurfaces and Light Blue on the undersurfaces. A Yellow identification band was applied to the nose and on the rear fuselage. The registration LG-2 was in Black. (Keski-Suomen Ilmailumuseo via Hannu Valtonen)

Conversion training was accompanied by such high attrition rate that the acronym "LaGG" began to take on another and more sinister connotation. Soviet Air Force pilots were suggesting that the acronym stood for *Lakirovanny Garantirovanny Grob*, or *Varnished Guaranteed Coffin*. Most pilots involved in the conversion cycle had flown the forgiving and extraordinarily maneuverable Polikarpov I-152 bi-plane. The LaGG-3, in contrast, was unforgiving, and was prone to an unheralded and vicious spin when engaged in a steep banking turn. It tended to nose-up during an approach and stalled at the least provocation. Conversion training with the LaGG-3 was seriously delayed because of the fact that a considerably number of LaGG-3s had to be returned to the factories for maintenance. The fighter suffered from many teething problems with the hydraulics installation. There were frequent landing gear failures, the brakes had a tendency to seize and the gun operating mechanism was unreliable. All of these problems had not been fully corrected by the Summer of 1941, when the Germans invaded the Soviet Union.

These shortcomings were considered so serious that the People's Commissariat for Aircraft Industry issued, on 31 May 1941, a special decree that, both, the flying characteristics of the fighter and production tempo should be improved immediately.

When the Germans launched Operation BARBAROSSA on 22 June 1941, only 322 LaGG-3 (1st Series versions) had left the four assembly lines. None of the fighters met the Luftwaffe during the first days of the invasion, because all serviceable LaGG-3 were assigned to Fighter Aviation Regiments in the Far Eastern Military Districts.

The Fighter Aviation Regiments equipped with LaGG-3s in the Far East remained on their bases until the moment it became clear to Stalin that the Japanese would respect the Japanese-Soviet neutrality pact signed on 13 April 1941 and would not attack the Soviet Union. Then all available LaGG-3s were immediately transferred to the Western front in order to rush them into combat against the Luftwaffe.

The LaGG-3 fighter had escaped notice by German intelligence until the type appeared for the first time on the battlefield in the Summer of 1941. The tight security measures of the Stalin administration in defense matters and a certain disinterest in new Soviet aircraft developments by the German intelligence services was generally responsible for this oversight. German intelligence rightly judged in May of 1941, a month before the invasion, that the Red Air Force was in a stage of re-equipping with new aircraft, which weakened it temporarily,

but there was no knowledge about the types of new aircraft going into service, such the Yak-1 and LaGG-3 fighters. The German Air Force 5th Division *Fremde Luftmächte Abteilung* intelligence service generally underestimated the strength of front-line Red Air Force regiments by some fifty percent. The German estimates for the aircraft production of the Soviet Union in 1941 was two thirds lower than the actual production figures in that year.

The fury of operation BARBAROSSA fell on the Soviet Air Force at the very moment a program had begun the re-equip forward air units with new generation combat aircraft. This transition was not advancing smoothly or quickly. Such programs inevitably brought disruption as air and ground crews were trained in the newer aircraft.

The LaGG-3 symbolized best the mixed characteristics of Soviet combat aircraft in 1941. With its wooden construction, the LaGG-3 bespoke of another era in aviation. While sturdy, the Soviet fighter demonstrated an unique and devastating blend of sluggishness and maneuverability.

During combat missions, many Soviet pilots flew with an open canopy and many aircraft had the canopy removed as a field modification. Early LaGG-3s could not jettison the canopy in case of an emergency and, in addition, the plexiglas from which it was manufactured, was almost as opaque as bottle glass, seriously impairing vision when the canopy was closed. Due to the additional drag caused by the open cockpit, the speed was reduced by some 9.3 mph (15 km/h). The view from the cockpit was regarded by many pilots as inadequate.

When LaGG-3 pilots met their enemies in the air for the first time they were badly trained and lacked initiative. Leaders were unable to command larger units, so when a Flight Leader was shot down, the rest of the flight lost their heads or continued to fly in formation without altering the direction until all of them were shot down.

Some skilled pilots, however, mastered the LaGG-3 and went on to score impressive victory tallies. One such pilot was Captain V. I. Popkov, later to emerge with forty-one kills as the Soviet Air Force's fifteenth-ranking ace, who scored his initial victories in a LaGG-3. Captain Popkov flew a total of 535 missions and was involved in 117 engagements with enemy aircraft over the Eastern front. Such pilots were the exception, however, and their skill had noth-

This 1st Series LaGG-3 was used in spin tests and had both wings tufted. The canopy was deleted on this aircraft and the rear glazing was replaced with metal. (Ivan Ivanov)

ing to do with the qualities of the LaGG-3.

During operations from unprepared fields, it was quite common to have the lower landing gear door removed from the main landing gear leg. This was to keep mud from building up on the landing gear.

LaGG-3 (1st Series) were usually camouflaged with Black-Green and Olive Green on the upper surfaces and Light Blue on the undersurfaces. The spinner was either painted in Light Blue, Silver or Black-Green, while the propeller was painted Black-Green.

The national markings were applied on the lower wing surfaces, but not on the upper wing surfaces. Most of the factories delivered early LaGG-3s with a Red star on the fuselage and on the tail, which were outlined in Black. Some LaGG-3 were painted with a large Red star on the rear fuselage and a small, unoutlined Red star on the rudder. While the most early LaGG-3s had all a small Black outlined Red star on the fuselage and the lower wing, some LaGG-3s, which were used in the Crimean sector, had small White outlined Red stars.

During the Winter of late 1941 and early 1942, a number of LaGG-3s were camouflaged with White paint on the upper surfaces. Only the national markings on the fuselage and the tactical number were not covered by the thick layers of whitewash paint. This temporary Winter camouflage resulted in a poor surface finish and reduced the aircraft's speed by some 6.2 mph (10 km/h).

During the Continuation War, the Finnish Air Force captured a LaGG-3 (1st Series) after it made a forced wheels-up landing on Finnish soil during early 1942. On 20 May 1942, the dismantled LaGG-3, Red 33, was transferred to a repair depot by truck.

Due to the extensive damage received during the forced landing, the repair work was not completed until 30 June 1944. The LaGG-3, now with the Finnish Air Force registration LG-2, was assigned to Hävittäjälentolaivue 32 - a fighter squadron being equipped with the

American built Curtiss Hawk 75A. The Hawk 75A was, at this time, inferior to modern Soviet fighter planes used in this theater of operations. The Finns, however, succeeded in downing several Pe-2s, LaGG-3s, MiG-3s and Yak-1s as well MBR flying boats. Skill and experience combined with the hardiness, airworthiness and sturdiness of the American fighter favored the Finns.

The mixed Curtiss and Lavochkin squadron was based at Nurmoila on the Olonets Isthmus and the Hawks frequently engaged Soviet flown LaGG-3s. In June 1942, five LaGG-3s were shot down and another four in July. On 5 September, the 2nd Flight attacked a large formation of forty Soviet aircraft. The battle took more than an hour and six LaGG-3s were shot down for no Finnish losses.

The captured LaGG-3 (LG-2) was camouflaged in Black and Olive Green on the uppersurfaces and Light Blue on the undersurfaces. A Yellow identification band was carried on the nose and on the rear fuselage. The undersides of the wing tips were also Yellow. The registration, LG-2, propeller, including the spinner, was in Black, while the tips of the propeller were in Yellow. Finnish Air Force national marking were applied on the rear fuselage and the wing upper and lower surfaces.

On 19 July 1944, the LaGG made a forced landing at Mensuvaara due to an engine malfunction. It was repaired, but was finally destroyed beyond repair on 30 August 1944, after the landing gear failed. The aircraft had logged a total of 26 hours and 35 minutes in Finnish Air Force service. Operation of the captured aircraft was often restricted by engine and gun malfunctions. Shortcomings which were also only too familiar in the Soviet Fighter Aviation Regiments.

LaGG-3 (4th Series)

Aircraft of the first three production series of the LaGG-3 were more or less identical, however, a number of changes were introduced on LaGG-3s built as part of the 4th Series. The changes were progressively introduced into the production lines of the four State Aircraft Factories.

The first LaGG-3s (4th Series) were very similar to the LaGG-3 of the preceding production batches. The LaGG-3 (4th Series) was powered by a Klimov M-105PA engine with the same horse power as the M-105P but with an improved K-105PB carburetor system and other minor detail changes.

The main change to the LaGG-3 (4th Series) was in the armament fitted. The Berezin UBS 12.7MM machine gun fitted between the cylinder blanks of the Klimov engine was replaced by a ShVAK 20MM cannon with 120 rounds. The first production versions of the LaGG-3 (4th Series), however, were still equipped with the Berezin UBS 12.7MM machine gun of the preceding LaGG-3 (1st Series) until sufficient quantities of cannon were available. Externally, the cannon could be identified by its heavier and longer muzzle.

The Soviet Union was, behind France, the second country to operationally adopt large caliber weapons for their fighters. The first fighter equipped with a 20MM cannon was the French-built Dewoitine D.510, which were used in combat during the Sino-Chinese war in May of 1938, operating from Yunnan. Soviet advisers and instructors in China quickly learned about the success of the large caliber weapons and this had a strong influence on the Soviet Air Force to fit their new fighters with cannons instead of machine guns. The Soviet Union also imported at least one D.510R from France for evaluation.

The ShVAK (*Shpitalny-Vladimirova Aviatsionnaya Krupnokalibernaya/Shpitalny-*

A very early LaGG-3 (4th Series) with oval wing root air intakes and two balance weights on the rudder. A very small Red star is carried on the tail and the aircraft has two tactical numbers, "White 50" on the fuselage and "Yellow 4" on the tail. (James V. Crow)

A LaGG-3 (4th Series) of the 82nd Fighter Aviation Regiment warms up its engine as it prepares for a mission in December of 1941. The tall antenna mast and the lack of the lower rudder balance weight on tail are identification features for the 4th Series LaGG-3. (Ivan Ivanov)

Development

LaGG-3 1st Series

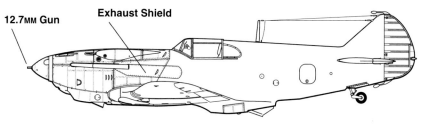

12.7MM Gun   Exhaust Shield

LaGG-3 4th Series

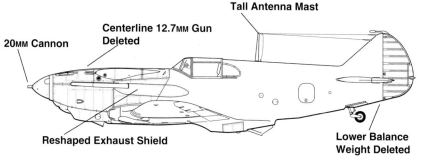

20MM Cannon   Centerline 12.7MM Gun Deleted   Tall Antenna Mast

Reshaped Exhaust Shield   Lower Balance Weight Deleted

Ground crewmen perform maintenance work on a LaGG-3 (4th Series) in the harsh winter conditions of early 1942. The aircraft was assigned to the defense of Moscow. The rectangular wing root air intakes were introduced on the 4th Series LaGG-3. (Ivan Ivanov)

This LaGG-3 (4th Series), Red 14, was captured by Slovakian soldiers during their quick advance into the Crimea. The aircraft is unusual in that it carried White outlined national markings. (Ivo Zetik)

A LaGG-3 (4th Series) is prepared for a test flight at the Test and Evaluation Center of the Luftwaffe at Rechlin, Germany. One captured LaGG-3 was used for a propaganda movie being produced at Rechlin in July of 1943. (Manfred Griehl)

Vladimirov - Large Caliber Cannon) was developed by Boris G. Shpitalny and S.V. Vladimirov on the principle of the highly successful 7.62MM ShKAS. The 20MM cannon had a rate of fire of 750 to 800 rounds per minute. LaGG-3s fitted with the cannon had the Berezin UBS 12.7MM machine gun, fitted on the centerline of the front fuselage, deleted, while the port side weapon was retained. This was one of several measures taken to reduce the aircraft's weight, which was increasing. LaGG-3s of the 1st Series had a gross weight of 7,376.5 pounds (3,346 kg), while LaGG-3s of the 4th Series weighed 7,231 pounds (3,280 kg).

The air intake on the starboard side of the nose, just behind the spinner, was deleted on the LaGG-3 (4th Series). Also deleted were the three vertical slots just below the exhausts. The air intake on the port side, just above the oil cooler intake was enlarged and an additional small intake was introduced.

The wing root air intakes were modified. On the LaGG-3 (1st Series) they were all oval in shape, but they became rectangular on the most LaGG-3 (4th Series) aircraft, however, the first fighters of the 4th Series were built with the oval air intakes.

The metal panel installed on the fuselage behind the exhaust stacks to protect the skinning from the hot exhaust gases was modified in shape. The metal panel was rounded at the rear on the LaGG-3 (1st Series), but was more conical on the LaGG-3 (4th Series). The horizontal fairing of the radiator outlet door had been reduced in size on the LaGG-3 (4th Series). 4th Series LaGG-3s also had the tall antenna mast used on very early 1st Series aircraft reintroduced.

Apart from the first production batches, the LaGG-3 (4th Series) had the lower balance weight on the rudder deleted. The LaGG-3 (1st Series) was equipped with small elevator trim tabs while the elevator tabs on the LaGG-3 (4th Series) were enlarged.

Due to the pressure of the Government to launch the LaGG-3 into mass production, the workmanship of the fighters produced after the beginning of the war was remarkable poorer

Finnish ski-troops gather around a downed LaGG-3 (4th Series, Serial 070171) which was hit by Finnish anti-aircraft fire over Nurmoila on 6 March 1942. At the time of the incident, the Lavochkin fighter was assigned to the 524th Fighter Aviation Regiment. The Finns decided that the fighter was damaged beyond economical repair during the crash landing and stripped it for usable parts. Some of its parts were used to keep three other LaGG-3s of the Finnish Air Force flying. (Keski-Suomen Ilmailumuseo via Hannu Valtonen)

(Right) The pilot of this early LaGG-3 (4th Series) crash landed in rather inaccessible terrain in the Northern sector of the Soviet Union, braking the fighter in half. The rectangular wing root air intakes identify this aircraft as a 4th Series LaGG-3. The spinner was painted White. (Ivan Ivanov)

This LaGG-3 (4th Series), Silver 71, had a Red star on the rear fuselage and on the fin/rudder. The tactical number, 71, was painted over the national marking on the tail. This particular aircraft, had unoutlined national markings, while most LaGG-3 carried Red stars with a Black outline. (Keski-Suomen Ilmailumuseo via Hannu Valtonen)

17

The port side console of a LaGG-3 (4th Series). The button on the control wheel is for the radio communication, while the three buttons inside the wheel are for the weapons. (Keski-Suomen Ilmailumuseo via Hannu Valtonen)

than the LaGG-3s built before the German invasion. This was also a result of insufficient training of the, for the most part, unskilled workers used to build LaGG-3s. Craftsmanship and fine tolerances were forgotten in the rush to produce as many LaGG-3s as possible after Hitler launched Operation BARBAROSSA. As a result, the performance and flying charac-

The pilot of this LaGG-3 of the 4th Series obviously tried to make a forced landing in rough terrain with the landing gear lowered and was obviously not successful. The aircraft has been torn in half just ahead of the fin and the forward portion has turned over. The two balance weights on the rudder were typical features of early production versions of the LaGG-3 (4th Series). (Ivan Ivanov)

The instrument panel of a LaGG-3 (4th Series). The PBP-1 gun sight is visible at the top of the panel. Most LaGG-3s had a White instrument panel with Black instruments. (Keski-Suomen Ilmailumuseo via Hannu Valtonen)

Red 29, a LaGG-3 (4th Series) was captured by the Finnish Air Force at Aunus during early 1942. It was transported by truck to a repair depot for rebuilding. The tactical number had been applied to the tail over the national marking. (Keski-Suomen Ilmailumuseo via Hannu Valtonen)

Red 29 was put up on jacks for inspection on 17 February 1942. The bent propeller blades indicate that the engine was still running when the pilot made a wheels up landing. Once repairs were completed, the LaGG-3 (4th Series) became LG-1 in Finnish Air Force service. (Keski-Suomen Ilmailumuseo via Hannu Valtonen)

This LaGG-3 of the 4th Series, formerly Red 29, was assigned to the LeLv 32 with the registration LG-1. The unit operated a total of three LaGG-3s, flying them alongside American-built Curtiss Hawk 75A fighters. The wing tips, nose and rear fuselage band were Yellow and the propeller was in Black. (Keski-Suomen Ilmailumuseo via Hannu Valtonen)

The Finnish LaGG-3 (4th Series) on the ramp at Utti Air Base in September of 1943. The LaGG-3s of LeLv 32 were intended to catch the fast Pe-2 bombers used for bombing missions over Finland. In the event, no Pe-2 were ever shot down by the Finnish flown LaGGs. (Keski-Suomen Ilmailumuseo via Hannu Valtonen)

The Finnish Air Force LaGG-3 (4th Series) parked outside a hangar at Tampere Air Depot with a captured Il-4 bomber in the background. The hangars were painted in camouflage colors to brake up their outline. (Keski-Suomen Ilmailumuseo via Hannu Valtonen)

LG-1 being refueled at Tampere during the Summer of 1943. The engine cowlings were removed so that ground crews could service the engine. (Keski-Suomen Ilmailumuseo via Hannu Valtonen)

The Finnish Air Force LaGG-3 (4th Series) at Tampere Air Depot during 1943. In order to avoid confusion with Soviet Air Force LaGG-3s, Finnish LaGG-3s had Yellow identification markings. (Keski-Suomen Ilmailumuseo via Hannu Valtonen)

Warrant Officer E. Koskinen in the cockpit of a Finnish LaGG-3. On 16 February 1944 Koskinen was ordered to attack of group of Soviet Pe-2 bomber, being escorted by two LaGG-3 fighters in the Kinkijeva area. During the dogfight that followed, he shot down one of the Soviet flown LaGG-3s while flying the LG-1. (Keski-Suomen Ilmailumuseo via Hannu Valtonen)

teristics of these LaGG-3s was inferior to those fighters produced before the war. The drag created by the poor craftsmanship of the skinning seriously affected the overall performance and flying characteristics of the LaGG-3.

A pre-war produced LaGG-3 (1st Series) had a speed of 357.2 mph (575 km/h), while a 4th Series LaGG-3 had a speed of 341 mph (549 km/h). A dramatic loss in rate of climb and ceiling was also noted. The LaGG-3 (1st Series) climbed at 2,412 feet per minute, while a 4th Series aircraft had a rate of climb of 1,930 feet per minute. Range dropped from 683.5 miles (1,100 km) to 540 miles (870 km) and the maneuverability also suffered. As a result of this loss of performance, the 4th Series LaGG-3 was no match for the Messerschmitt Bf-109F-4, the latest version of the Bf-109 deployed to the Eastern front.

On 4 July 1941, the State Defense Committee established a special Evacuation Council to supervise the removal of industries to areas behind the Ural mountains - well beyond the range of Luftwaffe bombers. Before this movement was completed in January of 1942, 1,523 factories, of which 1,360 were in defense manufacture, and 10 million workers and their families would be uprooted and transported more than 1,000 miles to the East. Because much of the aircraft industry was concentrated around Moscow, its evacuation did not get fully under way until the Autumn 1941, when the Soviet capital was clearly menaced.

OKB-301 was evacuated from Khimki, a Moscow suburb to GAZ-21 at Nizhny-Novgorod on the Volga river during the Autumn of 1941. The production facilities of GAZ-301, which produced the Yak-7, were transferred to Novosibirsk and combined with State Aircraft Factory 153. GAZ-31, a former Lebedev subsidiary and maritime aircraft production facility

Lieutenant V.A. Zaramenskikh in the cockpit of his LaGG-3 (4th Series) White 31. The tall antenna mast helps identify this LaGG as a 4th Series type fighter. The positioning of the tactical number in front of the unoutlined national marking is unusual. The first digit is slightly larger than the second. (Ivan Ivanov)

A White camouflaged early production LaGG-3 (4th Series) Red 46 being readied for a mission. The aircraft carries the insignia of a Guards Fighter Aviation Regiment above the fuselage national marking. The rudder trim tab on the rudder remained in Black Green. (Carl-Fredrik Geust)

before the war, was dismantled at Taganrog on the Sea of Azov and shipped south over the Caucasus mountains to Tbilisi, the capital of Georgia. Production of the LaGG-3 came to a halt at GAZ-23 in Leningrad after only sixty-five aircraft were completed. A short time before Leningrad was completely encircled by Axis troops, ninety-two large factories were evacuated using a force of some 60,000 railcars and trucks.

During 1941, a total of 2,463 LaGG-3s had left the four assembly lines, with some 2,141 LaGG-3s being built in the six months after the German attack to the Soviet Union. Of these, 1,659 were built at State Aircraft Factory 21. In addition, 474 were produced at GAZ-31, 265 at GAZ-153 and 65 at GAZ-23. The unit price of a LaGG-3 produced in 1941 was quoted at 310,000 Rubles.

Senior-Lieutenant P.P. Osipov in front of his nearly factory fresh LaGG-3 (4th Series) parked in a forward shelter made of trees during July of 1941. The Red Air Force was an expert in camouflage, successfully hiding their aircraft from the lenses of enemy reconnaissance aircraft. (Ivan Ivanov)

Senior-Lieutenant Georgi D. Kostylev on the wing of his White camouflaged LaGG-3 (4th Series) Red 35 discusses his last mission with a fellow pilot of the 3rd Guards Fighter Aviation Regiment, Baltic Fleet. (Carl-Fredrik Geust)

A single LaGG-3 of the 4th Series was captured by the Finnish Air Force during the Continuation War and repaired. This LaGG-3, Red 29, made a wheels up landing near Aunus

This LaGG-3 of the 6th Series was used for trials with the leading-edge automatic slats. With the exception of the repositioned pitot tube on the starboard wing leading edge, it was a standard production LaGG-3. (Ivan Ivanov)

A LaGG-3 (6th Series) assigned to the Flight Research Institute at Zhukovsky for trials with the leading-edge automatic slats, a feature which was later made standard on the 22nd Series LaGG-3. (Ivan Ivanov)

during early February of 1942 and it was dismantled and taken to a repair depot on 20 May 1942.

Red 29 became the first LaGG-3 in Finnish Air Force service and was assigned to LeLv 32 on 23 September 1942, with the registration LG-1, and it was usually assigned to Warrant Officer V. Ikonen. LeLv 32 was based at Nurmoila on the Olonets Isthmus as part of the 1st Flight Regiment, which was formed to conduct air operations on the Olonets Isthmus.

The LaGG-3 was intended to be used to intercept Pe-2 bombers on their bombing missions over Finland. The first combat flight was carried out on 23 March 1943 when a Pe-2 was chased, but not caught. In spite of several attempts during the Continuation War, the three Finnish Air Force LaGG-3s never succeeded in shooting down a Pe-2, which frequently penetrated Finnish air space.

Normally only one of the Finnish Air Force LaGG-3s was airworthy at one time, so flights were normally carried out alone. The only patrol flight conducted with two Finnish LaGG-3s (LG-1 and LG-3) was carried out on 27 October 1943. A dogfight with a Pe-2 bomber and two MiG-3 fighters ended without losses to either side.

On 4 November 1943, Lieutenant S. Alapuro returned from a mission with LG-1 and mistakenly retracted the landing gear on landing at Nurmoila. The pilot was not injured during the crash and the damaged LaGG-3 was again shipped to a repair depot.

After repair, LG-1 was again assigned to the LeLv 32. On 16 February 1944, Warrant Officer E. Koskinen was informed of an attack by a group of Pe-2 bombers, escorted by two LaGG-3 fighters, in the Kinkijeva area. In the dogfight that followed, one of the Soviet flown LaGG-3s was shot down by Warrant Officer E. Koskinen. On 4 September 1944, Finland sued for peace and an armistice was signed with the Soviet Union. Up to that time, the three Finnish Air Force LaGG-3s had made some forty-five combat flights. The last flight with LG-1 was on 23 January 1945, the fighter logged a total of 67 hours and 55 minutes while in Finnish service. On 1 April 1945, the Finnish national markings were changed to White/Blue/White roundels and even though both surviving LaGG-3s were in storage and non-operational, both were repainted with the new national markings.

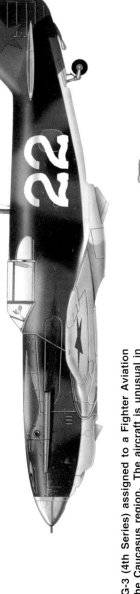

This LaGG-3 of the 1st Series was assigned to the 44th Fighter Aviation Regiment on the Leningrad Front during the Autumn of 1941

An early LaGG-3 (4th Series) assigned to a Fighter Aviation Regiment in the Caucasus region. The aircraft is unusual in that it carried two tactical numbers, White 50 and Yellow 4.

The Finnish Air Force captured this LaGG-3 (4th Series) and used it operationally. During February of 1944, Warrant Officer E. Koskinen shot down a Soviet LaGG-3 while flying this fighter.

This 4th Series LaGG-3 was assigned to a Fighter Aviation Regiment in the Crimea sector during 1942.

White 29, a LaGG-3 (29th Series), served in the Southern sector at Ostrogorsh. The aircraft was unusual in that it carried the tactical number forward of the national marking.

This LaGG-3 of the 29th Series carried the Kremlin style Red star on the fuselage.

A LaGG-3 of the 29th Series with a non-standard three digit tactical number on the fuselage and a second number on the fin.

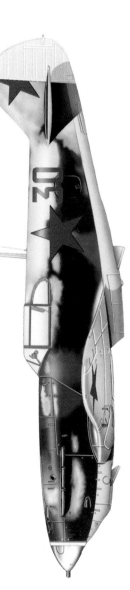

Red 30 was a LaGG-3 of the 35th Series. The aircraft's winter camouflage finish was badly weathered and there was only half a star on the fin.

White 24, a LaGG-3 of the 66th Series, was assigned to the 9th Fighter Aviation Regiment. It carried the late style national markings.

This LaGG-3 was captured and tested by the Japanese after its Soviet pilot defected in the Spring of 1942. The aircraft was flown from Mutanchiang Air Base in Manchuria.

LaGG-3 (8th Series)

LaGG-3s produced between the 4th and 7th Series were, apart from a few details and minor modifications, externally very similar to each other. Combat experience on the Eastern front against German fighters had shown that the firepower of the two ShKAS 7.62MM machine guns in the upper decking of the nose was insufficient to cause damage or to shoot down most German aircraft. Modern airwar clearly showed that larger caliber weapons, with a lower rate of fire, were superior to smaller, fast firing rifle caliber machine guns, such as the 7.62MM (approximately .30 caliber) weapons used on the early LaGG-3s. Small caliber guns usually caused only minor damage to an enemy aircraft, which, in many cases, allowed the enemy to survive the attack, be repaired and return to service. Large caliber weapons (12.7MM and above) used ammunition with explosive warheads that could cause severe damage to the airframe of an enemy and often set the fuel tanks on fire.

Since the LaGG-3 was by far the heaviest of the three modern fighters (Yak-1, MiG-3 and LaGG-3) in the inventory of the Soviet Air Force, a program was begun to reduce the weight

A LaGG-3 (8th Series) of the 5th Guards Fighter Aviation Regiment prepares for take off from a snow covered forward airfield during the Winter of 1942. The canopy was removed, a common practice with the LaGG-3. The aircraft in the background is a White winter camouflaged, ski-equipped LaGG-3, armed with RS-82 rockets under the wings. (Ivan Ivanov)

Armament Development

LaGG-3 (4th Series)

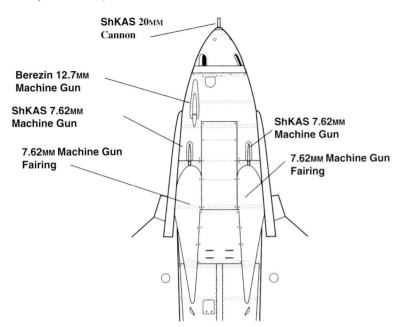

ShKAS 20mm Cannon

Berezin 12.7mm Machine Gun

ShKAS 7.62mm Machine Gun

7.62mm Machine Gun Fairing

ShKAS 7.62mm Machine Gun

7.62mm Machine Gun Fairing

LaGG-3 (8th Series)

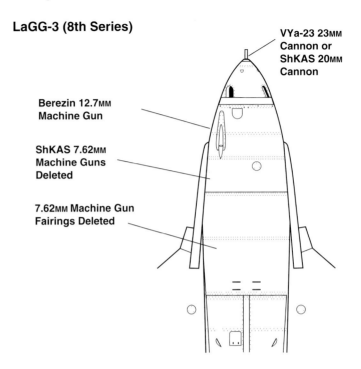

VYa-23 23mm Cannon or ShKAS 20mm Cannon

Berezin 12.7mm Machine Gun

ShKAS 7.62mm Machine Guns Deleted

7.62mm Machine Gun Fairings Deleted

of the LaGG-3. Since the two ShKAS 7.62MM guns were now considered more as additional weight than as efficient weapons, the OKB modified the forward fuselage area to delete these guns. This modification had to be introduced without causing any disruption to LaGG-3 production in any of the three factories, since every fighter was need to combat the Luftwaffe.

A LaGG-3 from the 8th Production Series was selected to serve as the prototype and was pulled from the production line and had the two ShKAS 7.62MM machine guns, their ammunition supply and upper fuselage fairings deleted. The armament configuration of a ShVAK 20MM cannon mounted between the engine cylinder banks and firing through the propeller hub augmented by a single Berezin UBS 12.7MM machine gun in the port upper nose became (with the exception of the 34th Series) standard for all later LaGG-3 versions until production was phased out. 8th Series LaGG-3s also had the oil cooler air intake on the nose slightly modified.

The first LaGG-3 (8th Series) aircraft were completed during late 1941. Some production batches of the LaGG-3 were equipped with the VYa-23 23MM cannon, replacing the ShVAK 20MM cannon between the engine cylinder banks. LaGG-3s fitted with the VYa-23 cannon did not receive a special designation, and some LaGG-3s of the 8th and later series could be fitted with either, the VYa-23 cannon and the ShVAK cannon, depending on availability.

The VYa-23 cannon had a muzzle velocity of 2,565 feet per second (905 meters per second) and a rate of fire between 370 and 500 rpm. LaGG-3s equipped with the VYa-23 cannon differed from the ShVAK armed versions in having a slightly longer cannon barrel, although

there were relatively few aircraft actually fitted with this weapon. The 23MM cannon was an effective weapon against light armor and soft skinned vehicles.

Some LaGG-3 were equipped with an AFA-1vertical camera mounted in the rear fuselage for reconnaissance duties. The camera had two different focal length lenses, one of 300MM and one of 500MM. During a mission, up to 150 seven inch by seven inch (18 x 18 cm) negatives could be exposed. The camera was operated by a 24 Volt electric motor, remotely operated by the pilot.

Combat for Soviet pilots flying the LaGG-3 during the early stages of the Great Patriotic War was disastrous. In front-line combat regiments, the LaGG-3 was openly referred to as a "morticians mate" and an aircraft whose intentions towards its pilots were as hostile as those of the Luftwaffe.

This censure of the LaGG-3 by its crews was not without some justification, since the fighter's performance and flight characteristics soon revealed the haste with which it had been tested and committed to production. The fighter was unforgivng to any but a highly-experienced pilot. It was a difficult machine to fly, since it was overweight, underpowered and possessed very unforgiving handling characteristics, especially stall characteristics. The average service pilots were not ready for a fighter with a high wing loading, being more used to the maneuverability and low wing loading of the earlier Polikarpov biplane fighters, such as the I-15 and I-153.

Japanese LaGG-3

The political climate between the Soviet Union and Japan was far from normal during the 1930s and early 1940s, and there were numerous border incidents along their mutual ill defined border areas. On 18 September 1931, Japan invaded Manchuria and assured the Soviet Union that this action would not touch the Eastern Chinese railway. The invasion ended on 18 February 1932 with a new state, Manchukno, being proclaimed as a Japanese puppet.

In January of 1934, Japanese troops attacking northern China moved through the Mongalian People's Republic. This action led to a military incident, because the Soviet Union felt that this was an invasion of an allied state. In June of 1937, the Soviet Union occupied two islands in the Amur River in Manchuria. Japan, occupying the opposite bank of the river, demanded their immediate evacuation. Border clashes in the area soon followed. When the Soviets finally withdrew, the Japanese, over Soviet protests, occupied the islands.

During the Lake Khasan incident of July 1938, Soviet air power came into sharp conflict with the Japanese. At Cheng Fu-keng Hill, the Soviet army built a fortification near the ill-defined Soviet-Korean border. In retaliation, the Japanese attacked, an effort which soon escalated the border dispute into a small-scale war. At the height of the conflict, the Soviets committed twenty-seven infantry battalions, supported by artillery and tanks. The Japanese withdrew from the disputed territory near Lake Khasan with significant losses. During the conflict the Soviets claimed more than 3,000 Japanese were either killed or wounded.

In May of 1939, a band of Mongolian nomads migrated east across the Khalkin-Gol River, but were driven back by border guards from the Japanese Kwantung Army. On 11 May, a full scale but undeclared war for a strip of arid pasture between the Khalkin-Gol river and the village of Nomonhan started between Imperial Japanese Army and the Soviet troops. The Red Army was superior to the Japanese Kwantung Army and on 16 September 1939 the two nations signed an armistice. The Japanese gained a respect for the Soviets, which added to their determination to stay out in the Great Patriotic War.

On 9 June 1940, both countries agreed to cease fighting on the Manchurian-Mongolian border. On 13 April 1941, a neutrality pact was signed between Stalin and the Japanese Foreign Minister Matsuoka.

In the Spring of 1942, a Soviet pilot defected with his LaGG-3 (8th Series) to Japanese occupied Manchukno and making a wheels-up landing in a field near Chiamus. This LaGG-3 previously belonged to a Fighter Aviation Regiment based in the Asian part of the Soviet Union. The LaGG-3 (8th Series) captured by the Japanese Kwantung Army was equipped with a VYa-23 23мм cannon and painted in the standard Soviet Air Force camouflage of Black-Green and Olive Drab uppersurfaces and Light Blue undersurfaces.

On 27 September 1942, after repairs had been completed, a number of evaluation flights began under the supervision of Major Yamamoto from the Army Air Test Center. During the trials, which were performed at Mutanchiang air base in Japanese occupied Manchukno, the LaGG-3 had the lower main wheel doors removed. The original pitot tube had been replaced by a larger Silver tube of Japanese origin. The propeller, remained in Natural Metal after its repair, with each tip being painted in Red. The original Soviet Air Force Red Stars were replaced by a Japanese Hinomaru. The fuselage marking had a White outline while the wing markings had no outline. The Red Star on the fin/rudder was simply overpainted.

The Japanese captured LaGG-3 on the ramp at Mutanchiang air base. The original pitot tube was replaced by a larger Silver tube of Japanese origin. The propeller was Natural Metal with Red tips. The lower main wheel doors were removed. (Heinz J. Nowarra)

The Japanese LaGG-3 in flight during the evaluation trials in the Autumn of 1942. The original Soviet Air Force Red Star was replaced by Japanese Hinomarus, the markings on the fuselage had a White outline, while the wing markings were not outlined. (Heinz J. Nowarra)

LaGG-3 (11th Series)

LaGG-3s built as part of the 11th Series were modified for the close support role with underwing bomb racks, rocket rails and provision for carrying drop tanks. A wet point for underwing fuel tanks was installed in each wing with the tank being suspended from a D3-40 bomb rack. The D3-40 was capable of carrying a 21 gallon (80 liter) drop tank. Apart from the provision for the D3-40 bomb rack and six Type RO-82 under wing rocket rails, LaGG-3s of the 11th Series were similar to aircraft built in the preceding series.

Another difference between earlier LaGG-3s and the most LaGG-3 (11th Series) aircraft was that the rear of the radiator fairing was enlarged and much more streamlined. Early LaGG-3 (11th Series) were still equipped with the older style rear radiator fairing typical for the preceding production batches.

The D3-40 bomb rack was also capable of carrying bombs up to 110 pounds (50 kg). Bomb types included the FAB-50 (FAB= *Fugasnaja Avia Bomba*/general purpose bomb) as well the AO-25M and the FAB-50M fragmentation bombs. The Soviet bombs were generally painted Gray with different color bands painted on the bombs to denote its purpose, however, these bands were not always applied. Anti-armor bombs had Yellow-Red bands, while fragmentation bombs had Green and Blue bands around the body. Practice bombs were painted White and Red. Beside the fragmentation and general purpose bombs, the LaGG-3 could also carry ZAB-50TG incendiary bombs, which were marked with Yellow and Blue bands.

Chemical weapons could also be carried, such as the ChAB-25 R-5 and the AOCh-15. The chemical agent was placed in ordinary fragmentation bombs shortly before a mission. The bombs containing chemical agents were marked with a Yellow-Blue band. There were two major types of chemical agents available, mustard gas and phosgene gas.

A White camouflaged LaGG-3 (11st Series) used on the Northern front in the Winter of 1942. The fighter was equipped with a D3-40 bomb rack, although no weapons were hung on the bomb rack. (Ivan Ivanov)

Development

LaGG-3 4th Series

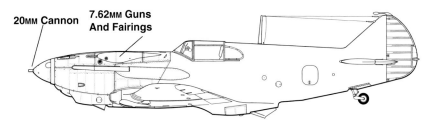

20MM Cannon
7.62MM Guns And Fairings

LaGG-3 11th Series

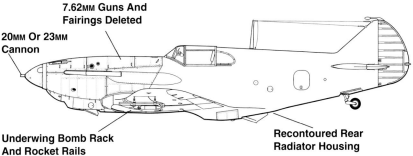

7.62MM Guns And Fairings Deleted
20MM Or 23MM Cannon
Underwing Bomb Rack And Rocket Rails
Recontoured Rear Radiator Housing

Beside chemical bombs the LaGG could carry a chemical agent dispenser VAP-6M (*Vylivnoj Aviazionnyj Pribor*/Chemical Aviation Container) under each wing. The VAP-6M could carry up to 10 gallons (38 liters) of mustard or phosphorus gas. The gas was dispensed through an ASBR-2 dispenser system, which allowed either or both tanks to be used. It took three to four second to dispense the chemical agents from the tanks over enemy troops.

Using the same container as for chemical agents, a liquid fire dispenser ZAP-6 (*Zashigatelnyj Aviazionnyj Pribor*/Liquid Fire Aviation Container) had been developed for use on close support aircraft. Under the container a second, smaller container of hydrogen sulfide was added to ignite the phosphors when it left the upper container.

During early 1942, the LaGG-3 was increasingly employed in the low-level close-support and ground attack role, where its ability to absorb considerably battle damage was appreciated. The LaGG-3 saw considerably action in the close support role during the battle of Moscow on the Kalinin Front in late 1941 and early 1942. The 129th Fighter Aviation Regiment, flying LaGG-3s, was awarded Guards Regiment status for their actions. On 6 December 1941, the former 129th Fighter Aviation Regiment became the 5th Guards Fighter Aviation Regiment.

LaGG-3s of the 11th Series were equipped with three RO-82 rocket rails under each wing

Rocket Armament

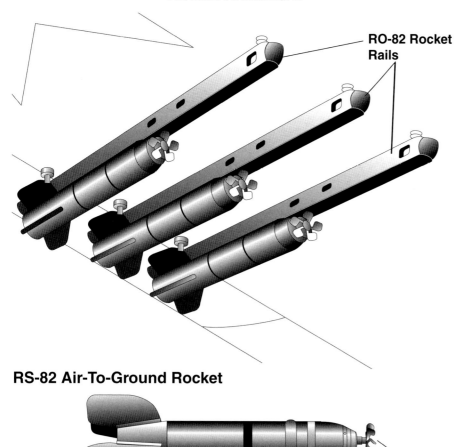

RO-82 Rocket Rails

RS-82 Air-To-Ground Rocket

Arming Vanes

for RS-82 (RS = *Raketnij Snarjad*/Rocket projectile) unguided air-to-ground rockets. These did impact on performance and, when six RS-82 rockets were carried, top speed was decreased by about 15.5 mph (25 km/h). The rockets were aiming using the standard PBP-1 gunsight.

In early 1942 the improved RS-132 unguided rocket became available in quantity. The RS-132 could be carried on the same rocket rails as the RS-82. Both the RS-82 and RS-132 could knock out light and medium tanks, but because of the fact that they were highly inaccurate, the rockets were usually used to attack tight columns and concentrations of armored equipment.

During the Winter of 1942, a number of LaGG-3 (11th Series) were equipped with a non-

A line-up of ski-equipped LaGG-3s (11th Series) during an inspection. All the aircraft were painted with a crudely applied Winter camouflage. (Robert Bock)

These LaGG-3s (11st Series) are having their standard wheel landing gear replaced by skis for operations from snow. The aircraft in the foreground has the port wheel removed from the landing gear leg, while the aircraft in the background still has its wheels. (Robert Bock)

31

Captain V.P. Mironov in the cockpit of his LaGG-3 (11st Series) in the Summer of 1942. Captain Mironov shot down twenty-one enemy aircraft and became a Hero of the Soviet Union. A number of LaGG-3 (11th Series) had the air intakle on the nose deleted. (Ivan Ivanov)

retractable ski undercarriage, in place of the main wheels. While allowing operations from show covered fields, the additional drag of the skis reduced the aircraft's speed and worsened already difficult handling qualities. As a result, the skis were replaced by the standard wheel configuration as soon the weather conditions permitted.

This Winter camouflaged LaGG-3 (11st Series) crash landed in the Baltic region of the Eastern Front in the Winter of 1942. There are Type RO-82 rocket rails installed under the wing. (Ivan Ivanov)

D3-40 Bomb Rack

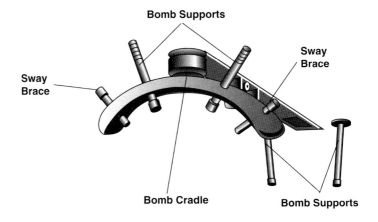

Bomb Supports

Sway Brace

Sway Brace

Bomb Cradle

Bomb Supports

LaGG-3 (23rd Series)

The LaGG-3 (23rd Series) differed from previous production batches in that it had a modified rudder. While LaGG-3s up to the 22nd Series had a straight rudder, the LaGG-3 (23rd Series) had a bend at the top of the rudder.

The first production batches of LaGG-3 (23rd Series) were equipped with a balance weight on the modified rudder, but most 23rd Series LaGG-3s had the balance weight deleted.

A few LaGG-3 (23rd Series) were re-equipped with the VISh-105SV propeller. These new propellers differed from the standard VISh-61P propeller in having an enlarged spinner. The 23rd Series was produced until the Summer 1942.

Some LaGG-3s (23rd Series) had a modified exhaust collector tube, with a bend to the side at the end of the exhaust tube to deflect hot exhaust away from the fuselage skinning. These LaGG-3s lacked the fuselage protective plate normally installed just behind the exhausts.

In early 1942, it became clear that the LaGG-3 was in many respects inferior to the Yak-1 and Yak-7. The Yakovlev designs were superior in performance and were much easier to produce than the LaGG-3 with its Delta-Wood structure. As a result, the Commissariat of the People for the Aviation Industry ordered that GAZ-153 should convert from LaGG-3 produc-

A ski equipped LaGG-3 of the 23rd Series with no tactical markings. A typical feature of the LaGG-3 (23rd Series) was the lack of the balance weights on the rudder tip and the enlarged rudder with a bend. (Nigel Eastaway/RART)

Development

LaGG-3 (11th Series)

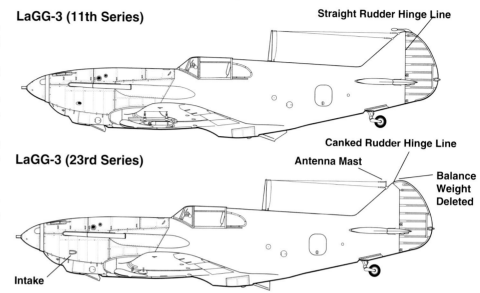

Straight Rudder Hinge Line

Canked Rudder Hinge Line

Antenna Mast

Balance Weight Deleted

LaGG-3 (23rd Series)

Intake

33

This 23rd Series LaGG-3 is configured with RO-82 rocket rails under each wing for the ground attack role. These rails could carry either the RS-82 of RS-132 air-to-ground unguided rocket, either of which was capable of knocking out enemy armor. (Nigel Eastaway/RART)

tion to the Yak-7 fighter. At that time, the factory had produced a total of 330 LaGG-3s. GAZ-21 converted to the radial engined La-5 in the Autumn of 1942, and for a while both, LaGG-3s and La-5s were produced at the factory. As a result, GAZ-31 became the sole factory building LaGG-3s.

During 1942, a total of 2,771 LaGG-3 were built, more than in any other year the LaGG-3 was in production.

This ski equipped LaGG-3 of the 23rd Series has the enlarged rudder which was standard for this series of LaGG-3s. This is an early production aircraft still fitted with the rudder balance weight used on previous models. The large spinner for the VISh-105SV propeller is non-standard. (Nigel Eastaway/RART)

This LaGG-3 (23rd Series) was fitted with two 21 gallon (80 liter) drop tanks attached to the under wing D3-40 bomb racks. There are also three RO-82 rocket rails with RS-82. (Ivan Ivanov)

This ski-equipped LaGG-3 of the 23rd Series had a non standard exhaust collector tube that is bent on the end to deflect the hot exhaust gases away from the fuselage. The standard fuselage metal plate has been deleted. (Nigel Eastaway/RART)

LaGG-3 (29th Series)

The LaGG-3 (29th Series) differed from earlier variants in that it was equipped with a more powerful 1, 210 hp Klimov M-105PF engine. This engine produced about 110 hp more than the Klimov M-105PA engine used on the previous production batches of the LaGG-3. The power, however, was increased at expense of its altitude rating. While the M-105PA performed well up to altitudes of 13,123 feet (4,000 meters) the M-105PF had its best performance up to 8,858 feet (2,700 meters). Combat experience had shown, however, that most combat on the Eastern Front was at low altitudes.

Externally, the LaGG-3s of the 29th Series had the large, single exhaust collector tube replaced by three individual exhaust stubs located on each side of the nose. In addition, the protective cover plate behind the exhaust collector tube was deleted. Apart from these two features, the LaGG-3 (29th Series) were nearly identical to the previous production batches.

The first LaGG-3 of the 29th Series were delivered from GAZ-21 and GAZ-31 in June of 1942. There were only a few 29th Series LaGG-3s built at State Aircraft Factory 21 before production switched to the radial engined La-5.

One of the first LaGG-3 (29th Series) production examples was assigned in the same month for test trials to the Scientific Research Institute of the Soviet Air Force at Sverdlovsk. The LaGG-3 had, due to its reduced armament, a take off weight of 6,966 pounds (3,160 kg) while the 4th Series LaGG-3 had a weight of 7,231 pounds (3,280 kg). With its improved low

A LaGG-3 (29th Series), White 25, captured by advancing German troops on the Eastern front. The fighter carried a Red-Black Kremlin star national marking on the fuselage and a small Red star on the tail. (Frieder Voigt)

Development

LaGG-3 (23rd Series)

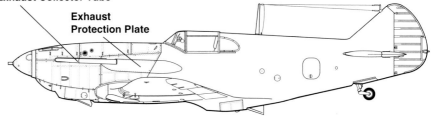

Exhaust Collector Tube

Exhaust Protection Plate

LaGG-3 (29th Series)

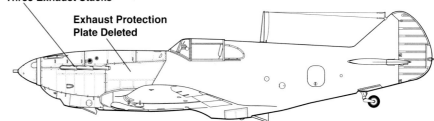

Three Exhaust Stacks

Exhaust Protection Plate Deleted

This LaGG-3 (29th Series) carried a crudely painted Red star on the tail and none of the national markings were outlined. The three digit tactical number, White 229, was unusual for an aircraft assigned to a Fighter Aviation Regiment. Additionally, a small White 8 was on the rudder. (Manfred Griehl)

This Winter camouflaged LaGG-3 (29th Series), Red 27, was equipped with a VISh-105SV propeller, identified by the large spinner. This type of spinner is a non-standard feature of aircraft of the 29th series. (Manfred Griehl)

A line-up of LaGG-3s of the 29th Series. The aircraft in the foreground carried a White bird silhouette as a personal marking and a White spinner. The small three exhaust stubs on the LaGG-3 (29th Series) differed from earlier LaGG-3s which used a single exhaust collector tube. (Robert Bock)

This LaGG-3 (29th Series) was captured by Hungarian troops at Ostrogorsh in the Ukraine. The position of the tactical number, White 29, in front of the national marking was unusual. A White band was painted on the Black-Green spinner. (Attila Bonhardt/Hungarian War Archive)

altitude M-105PF engine, the LaGG-3 (29th Series) had a speed of 315 mph (507 km/h) at sea level, 19.2 mph (31 km/h) faster than the LaGG-3 (4th Series). The LaGG-3 (29th Series) had a maximum speed of 351 mph (566 km/h) and a rate of climb of 2,563 feet per minute.

Some late production batches of the LaGG-3 (29th Series) were equipped with an enlarged radiator, with the radiator intake being more rectangular in shape.

Beginning in August of 1942, the original RSI-3 radio was replaced by a short-wave RSI-4 *Malyutka* receiver. In contrast to the RSI-3 which had five pre-fixed frequencies, the RSI-4 had the capability of using variable frequencies in a band between 3.7 and 6.05 Megacycles.

A few late production batches of the LaGG-3 (29th Series) versions were equipped with the VISh-105SV propeller, although, this type of propeller was not introduced on a large scale until the 33rd Series.

A LaGG-3 (29th Series) and two Lend-Lease Hawker Hurricane IIBs awaiting shipment to Hungary at an Ukrainian railway station. The aircraft were captured at different locations on the Southern Front by advancing Hungarian troops and were sent back for testing. (George Punka)

LaGG-3 (33rd Series)

The 33rd Series LaGG-3 differed very little from the 29th Series. The main difference was that the VISh-105SV propeller and slightly larger spinner became standard.

The tailplane was also modified on the LaGG-3 (33rd Series). Previous production batches had a rounded rudder with a straight hinge line, while LaGG-3 (33rd Series) had a slightly pointed fin and rudder with improved hinges.

LaGG-3 (34th Series) - Anti-tank Variant

The LaGG-3 (34th Series) was modified to serve as an anti-tank ground attack aircraft. The standard ShVAK 20MM cannon was replaced by a NS-37 37MM cannon with an ammunition supply of twenty rounds and a rate of fire of 250 rounds per minute. Externally, the LaGG-3 (34th Series) could be identified from the preceding 33rd Series and later LaGG-3s by the longer cannon barrel of the 37MM cannon. The port Berezin UBS 12.7MM gun was retained.

The first examples of the NS-37 cannon were available in the Autumn of 1942 and after a series of tests with the new weapon, some forty LaGG-3 (34th Series) were sent to Stalingrad for front-line evaluation with the new armament.

Combat experience clearly showed that the LaGG-3 was not well suited for the anti-tank role. The flying characteristics of the cannon armed LaGG-3 were even worse that the standard LaGG-3 since the center of gravity had shifted. The recoil forces of the cannon were

Warming up the Klimov M-105PF engine on an early LaGG-3 (35th Series), Red 52, of the 3rd Guards Fighter Aviation Regiment. The enlarged, more rectangular radiator fairing under the fuselage was a change from earlier production variants of the LaGG-3. (Ivan Ivanov)

severe and led to fuselage damage. Additionally, the Il-2 Type 3M performed much better in the anti-tank role armed with two NS-37 cannons in underwing gondolas. As a result, there was only one LaGG-3 production batch built with this armament configuration.

Cannon armed LaGG-3s intended for anti-tank missions were not new. In August of 1941, three LaGG-3 (1st Series) were equipped with a Sh-37 37MM cannon and immediately sent to the front, where they were employed with a some success.

LaGG-3 (35th Series)

The LaGG-3 (35th Series) incorporates a number of changes aimed at improving the flying characteristics of the fighter, especially during take off and landing. Service pilots generally found the LaGG-3 to be a difficult machine to fly. It tended to nose-up during an approach and stall at the least provocation.

As a result, automatic slats were introduced on the wing leading edge to improve stall characteristics. As a result, the starboard pitot tube was enlarged and repositioned under the wing leading edge. The slats had been successfully tested on LaGG-3s built as part of the 22nd Series with full scale production introduced on LaGG-3s of the 34th Series.

The early LaGG-3 (35th Series) had a smaller spinner on the VISh-105SV propeller, but the most fighters built in this series had an enlarged, more pointed spinner, which became standard.

In contrast to the previous production batches, the LaGG-3 (35th Series) had an enlarged radiator and, as a result, the radiator fairing became larger and more squared than on the previous production models.

A early LaGG-3 of the 35th Series prepares to take-off on a mission. The early production examples of this series were equipped with a smaller, less pointed spinner than the standard production 35th Series LaGG-3. The rudder of this Winter camouflaged LaGG-3 Red 30, was a replacement from another aircraft that did not carry the national marking. (Ivan Ivanov)

Camouflaged with foliage, this late production LaGG-3 (35th Series) was refueled on an airstrip on the Kalinin front in May of 1943. The air intake just above the wing root was a feature found on late production LaGG-3s. (Ivan Ivanov)

The LaGG-3 (35th Series) was also modified with a retractable tail wheel, which had been tested on a small number of aircraft built in the 28th Series. The first LaGG-3 (35th Series) were fitted with small, flush type retractable tailwheel doors. These were replaced on most 35th Series aircraft by enlarged, bulged tailwheel doors.

The 35th Series LaGG-3s also had the air intake located below the exhaust stubs reduced in size and reshaped. In addition, late production batches of the LaGG-3 (35th Series) had an air intake behind the exhaust stubs, a feature which became standard on later LaGG-3s built in

Final assembly of LaGG-3s (35th Series) is ongoing (in the foreground) while their replacement, the La-5 is assembled in the background at State Aircraft Factory 31 in the Autumn of 1942. The slats on the aircraft in the foreground were painted before the camouflage was applied to the fighter. (Ivan Ivanov)

A LaGG-3 (35th Series) being refueled at an airstrip on the Eastern front. The fuel capacity of the LaGG-3 was 127 gallons (480 liters) distributed between five tanks. The large spinner for the VISh-105SV propeller was a good identification feature for the 35th Series aircraft. (Ivan Ivanov)

Wing Development

LaGG-3 (29th Series)

Hard Wing Leading Edge With No Wing Slat

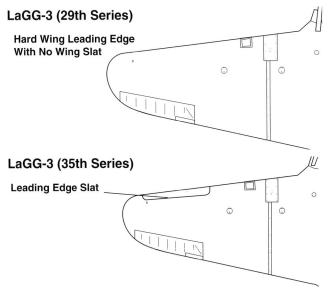

LaGG-3 (35th Series)

Leading Edge Slat

Finnish Air Force personnel look over a crash landed LaGG-3. The inspection team went over the fighter carefully to decide if it could be salvage or if it should be stripped of usable parts. In the event, the team decided that the aircraft could be put back into service. (Keski-Suomen Ilmailumuseo via Hannu Valtonen)

On 14 September 1942, Soviet and Finnish fighters clashed over the Finnish held Olonets Isthmus. One LaGG-3 (35th Series) was damaged by Altto Tervo and belly landed in a meadow at Ala-Sedoksa, where it drew considerably attention from the local habitants. The muzzle for the Berezin UBS 12.7MM machine gun is clearly visible. (Keski-Suomen Ilmailumuseo via Hannu Valtonen)

The LaGG-3 (Serial 3121357), captured by the Finnish Air Force left the factory on 11 August 1942 and had been in front line service for a short time. The Finns considered the LaGG-3 as repairable and it was taken to a repair depot for rebuilding. (Keski-Suomen Ilmailumuseo via Hannu Valtonen)

43

LG-3 undergoes repair at the Mechanic's School at Utti Air Base during 1944. Visible in the background is the wing of a captured Lend-Lease P-40M Warhawk, White 23. The Curtiss fighter became KH-51 in the Finnish Air Force, after it made a forced landing in Finland on 27 December 1943. (Keski-Suomen Ilmailumuseo via Hannu Valtonen)

the 66th Series.

The LaGG-3 (35th Series) variants were produced from August of 1942 until Spring of 1943 at GAZ-31, which became the sole State Aircraft Factory building LaGG-3s in 1943.

Although the LaGG-3 was regarded as obsolete by the NKAP (Commissariat of the People for the Aviation Industry) in early 1942, production continued until preparations were finished to convert the production lines to more advanced fighters. Up to the end of 1942, 2,771 LaGG-3 had left the assembly lines, more than in any other year the type was produced.

Finnish LaGG-3 (35th Series)

Major Aulis Bremer, commander of LeLv 32, at the controls of the Finnish Air Force LaGG-3 (35th Series), LG-3. All LaGG-3s equipped with slats had the pitot tube relocated under the wing leading edge. (Keski-Suomen Ilmailumuseo via Hannu Valtonen)

LG-3 taxies out for a mission at Tampere Air Force Base in January of 1943. The Finnish national markings were applied on the wing surfaces and the fuselage. The two Yellow bands, were recognition markings to help distinguish LG-3 from Soviet operated LaGG-3s in the area. (Keski-Suomen Ilmailumuseo via Hannu Valtonen)

Ground crew of the LeLv 32 push the LaGG-3 (LG-3) into a wooden shelter at Nurmoila Air Base on the Olonets Isthmus. All Finnish flown LaGG-3s had the tips of the propeller blades painted Yellow. (Keski-Suomen Ilmailumuseo via Hannu Valtonen)

During the Summer of 1944, LG-3 was equipped with a short antenna mast, similar to early LaGG-3s. The upper portion of the Yellow nose identification band was overpainted in Olive-Green. (Keski-Suomen Ilmailumuseo via Hannu Valtonen)

LG-3 was the only Finnish flown LaGG-3 to carry the small Red cross marking, noting the location of the first aid kit, on the fuselage just above the Black LG-3 registration. (Keski-Suomen Ilmailumuseo via Hannu Valtonen)

On 1 April 1945, the national markings of the Finnish Air Force were changed to White/Blue/White roundel. The two remaining LaGG-3, at that time in storage at Tampere Air Depot, received the new marking, which were considerably smaller then the old markings. No flights were ever made in these markings. (Keski-Suomen Ilmailumuseo via Hannu Valtonen)

On 14th September 1942, Soviet and Finnish fighters clashed together over the Finnish held Olomets Isthmus. A LaGG-3 (35th Series) was shot up by a Finnish Air Force pilot, Altto Tervo and belly landed with only minor damage in a meadow at Ala-Sedoksa. Apart from a bent VISh-105SV propeller, there was only minor damage done to the fuselage. A salvage team dismantled the fighter and shipped it to a repair depot, where the Soviet fighter arrived on 7 October 1942. After repairs, the aircraft was assigned to LeLv 32 with the registration LG-3.

On 7 July 1943, the port wing and the propeller were damaged on take-off from Nurmoila but the aircraft was soon repaired. During the overhaul, the radio antenna was shortened to the same size as the radio antenna of LG-2.

The last flight of LG-3 was on 29 January 1945, this was also the last flight of a LaGG-3 in Finnish Air Force service. The fighter was stored at Tampere Air Depot after a total flight time of 79 hours and 40 minutes, more than any other LaGG-3 in Finnish Air Force service.

LG-3 was camouflaged in Black and Olive Green on the uppersurfaces and Light Blue undersurfaces. It differed from the other two Finnish LaGGs in that a Red cross in a White disc was added above the registration on the port side, indicating the location of a small first aid kit. In 1944, the upper part of the Yellow nose band on LG-3 was overpainted with Olive Green, while the lower half remained Yellow.

LaGG-3 (66th Series)

The LaGG-3s of the 66th Series were to become the last liquid cooled, in-line engined fighters built by Lavochkin. Compared with previous versions, the 66th Series aircraft had a considerable airframe weight reduction. And, although additional weight was saved by elimination of certain items of equipment, the power to weight ratio of the 66th Series fighters was by far the lowest of all Soviet Air Force fighter aircraft produced at that time. While the LaGG-3 (29th Series) had a take off weight of 6,966 pounds (3,160 kg), the LaGG-3 (66th Series) weighed in at 6,611 pounds (2,990 kg), some 385 pounds less. Series production of this aircraft was launched at GAZ-31 and this State Aircraft Factory became the sole plant producing the LaGG-3 during 1943.

The LaGG-3 (66th Series) had a number of aerodynamic refinements over its predecessors. Production of this last production batch of the Klimov engined LaGG-3 was launched exclusively at GAZ-31, located in Tbilisi, the capital of the Georgian Soviet Socialist Republic. In the 1940s, Georgia had enhanced political significance, since it was the birthplace of the Soviet Leader Iosif Stalin. This last production batch was being built side by side with the next generation radial-engined La-5 and a number of features and improvements from the La-5 versions were also adopted for the 66th Series LaGG-3. The La-5, however was never produced in substantial number at GAZ-31. In 1942, only twenty-two of the radial engined fighters were produced and only a handful were built during 1943, so that GAZ-31 concentrated nearly its entire production on the LaGG-3. When the last LaGG-3 left the assembly line, production of Lavochkin fighters was stopped at that State Aircraft Factory. After a reorganization, the plant subsequently built Yakovlev Yak-3 fighters with a total of 1,008 being built at the plant.

Evaluation trials performed by test pilots of the Scientific Research Institute of the Soviet Air Force at Sverdlovsk, East of the Ural mountains, clearly showed that the Series 66 LaGG-3 had superior performance to any previous production variants of the LaGG-3. The LaGG-3 (66th Series) reached a speed of 336 mph (542 km/h) at sea level while the earlier LaGG-3

A line-up of 66th Series LaGG-3s of the 9th Fighter Aviation Regiment of the Black Sea Fleet. Each propeller blade has been painted with a White stripe. The small antenna mast and the four exhaust stubs were identification features for the last production version of the LaGG-3. (Ivan Ivanov)

This LaGG-3 (66th Series) is suspended from a special rack while undergoing structural tests at the TsAGI (Central Aero Hydrodynamics Institute). The lack of a landing light under the port wing and the small radiator fairing were features of the last production batch of LaGG-3s. (Nigel Eastaway)

Fuselage Development

LaGG-3 (35th Series)

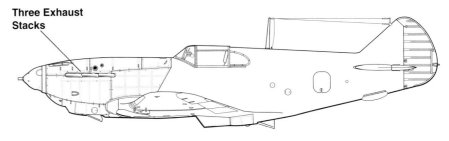

Three Exhaust Stacks

LaGG-3 (66th Series)

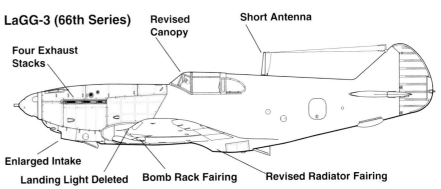

Revised Canopy   Short Antenna

Four Exhaust Stacks

Enlarged Intake

Landing Light Deleted   Bomb Rack Fairing   Revised Radiator Fairing

(29th Series) could only reach a speed of 315 mph (507 km/h). A top speed of 367 mph (591 km/h) was recorded at altitude, which was some 15.5 mph (25 km/h) faster than on previous production version of the LaGG-3. The LaGG-3 (66th Series) was, however, remarkable slower than the primary enemy fighter on the Eastern Front at that time, the Messerschmitt Bf-109G-6, which had a top speed of 391 mph (630 km/h). The German fighter was also more heavily armed. Its armament included a MG-151 20MM cannon and two MG-131 13MM machine guns mounted in the cowl. The LaGG-3 (66th Series) was also an easy pray for the Focke-Wulf Fw-190 A-3 which had a top speed of 410 mph (660 km/h).

The LaGG-3 (66th Series) had a rate of climb of 2,929 feet per minute, while the LaGG-3 (29th Series) had a rate of climb of 2,563 feet per minute. The ceiling of the LaGG-3 (66th Series) was reduced to 31,496 feet (9,600 meters), which was 1,312 feet (400 meters) lower then on previous production versions. Due to the weight reduction program, the LaGG-3 (66th Series) was a highly maneuverable fighter, and was the most maneuverable of any production series.

The first LaGG-3 (66th Series) were produced during the Spring of 1943. The entire nose was modified, using data suppled by the specialists of the Central Aero Hydrodynamics Institute at Zhukovsky. They incorporated a number of changes which were also made to the Yakovlev Yak-1B to improve the aircraft's streamlining and to reduce drag. Many of the detail changes on the LaGG-3 (66th Series) were similar to those made to the Yak-1B nose, including the redesigned oil cooler intake and the exhaust stub configuration.

Under the nose, the oil cooler intake was enlarged and reshaped so that it was now slanted forward. The rear engine cowling panel behind the exhaust stubs was also slightly changed in shape, when compared with the panels used on all previous LaGG-3 versions. The air intake under the exhaust stubs was enlarged and moved slightly to the rear. In addition, a second air intake was added on the fuselage, above the wing roots.

The three large exhaust stubs were changed to four smaller exhaust stubs and a fairing was added to the fuselage above the exhausts. The landing light on the port wing was deleted, so that the LaGG-3 (66th Series) had no landing lights. The rectangular wing root air intakes were reshaped, becoming oval in shape.

The underwing bomb rack was streamlined by the addition of a tear drop shaped fairing. The radiator fairing under the fuselage was reduced in size and reshaped, returning to the same size as the radiator used on early production LaGG-3s.

The cockpit windshield used on the La-5 was adopted for use on the 66th Series LaGG-3. The round frame for the windshield was changed to a rectangular shaped frame in order to accommodate a 55MM section of armor glass mounted behind the windshield. An additional frame was also added to the windshield. Early production versions of the LaGG-3 lacked armor glass behind the windscreen and had only one frame on the windscreen. The rear frame of the aft sliding canopy was enlarged and had a small vent window installed in it.

The first production versions 0f the LaGG-3 (66th Series) were delivered with the tall radio mast adopted from the LaGG-3 (35th Series), however, the most LaGG-3 (66th Series) built were fitted with a smaller radio antenna mast.

The last LaGG-3s (66th Series) was delivered in September of 1943 from State Aircraft 31. When production ceased, a total of 6,528 LaGG-3 of sixty-six different production batches had left the four State Aircraft Factories between January of 1941 and September of 1943. In the last year of production, a total of 1,294 LaGG-3 were delivered from the State Aircraft Factory at Tbilisi.

These LaGG-3 were involved, during April and May of 1943, in the battle of Kuban in the North Caucasus area. It was in this area that the Luftwaffe and the Red Air Force fought one of the most dramatic air battles of the Great Patriotic War, which became an important bench mark for the Red Army. Along with other formations involved in the campaign, there was a squadron of 66th Series LaGG-3s acquired from funds collected in the Georgian Soviet Socialist Republic. These LaGG-3s were assigned to the 88th Fighter Aviation Regiment.

The LaGG-3 (66th Series) served well into 1944 in various Red Air Force units, including the 9th Fighter Aviation Regiment of the Black Sea Fleet, which operated the fighter in the Novorossijsk area during the Spring of 1944. In May of the same year, the formation was transferred to the Baltic Fleet as part of the 11th Ground Attack Division. These LaGG-3 then took part in the major attacks against the Finnish forces on the Karelian Isthmus in June of 1944.

66th Series LaGG-3s were delivered in the standard Soviet camouflage of Black-Green and Olive-Green on the uppersurfaces and Light Blue undersurfaces. Most of these aircraft had a large, small Black outlined Red star on the fuselage and the lower wing. A small Red star was added on the tail.

Beginning in early 1944, a new style of national marking was introduced. The Red star was given a thick White outline and a thin Red outline. LaGG-3s which remained in service at that time were repainted with these new national markings applied. The small Red star on the tail, however, remained unchanged or was overpainted.

This aircraft served as a testbed for the LaGG-3 (66th Series). It was a LaGG-3 (4th Series) fuselage mated with a Klimov M-105PF engine and a slatted wing. The fighter carried the new, oval shaped air intakes in the wing roots, but was still equipped with a landing light, which was deleted on production 66th Series LaGG-3s. (Nigel Eastaway)

An very early LaGG-3 (66th Series) during the evaluation trials. It differed from later standard production fighters of this series in that it was still equipped with the tall antenna mast used on the previous production batches. (Ivan Ivanov)

A LaGG-3 (66th Series) with a Lend-Lease Curtiss P-40 in the background. This fighter carried the new national markings introduced during early 1944. The small Red star on the tail remained in its original configuration while the fuselage and wing stars had the White and Red outlines. (S.H.A.A.)

Russian Aircraft Of The Second World War

1155

1157

1162

From

squadron/signal publications